The Little Camel and the Christmas Star:

A Heartwarming Nativity Story for Kids
(Ages 4-8)

Tiina Hoddy

© Copyright Tiina Hoddy 2025 - All rights reserved.

The content within this book may not be reproduced, duplicated or transmitted without direct written permission from the author or the publisher. Under no circumstances will any blame or legal responsibility be held against the publisher, or author, for any damages, reparation, or monetary loss due to the information contained within this book. Either directly or indirectly. You are responsible for your own choices, actions, and results.

Legal Notice:

This book is copyright protected. This book is only for personal use. You cannot amend, distribute, sell, use, quote or paraphrase any part, of the content within this book, without the consent of the author or publisher.

Disclaimer Notice:

Please note the information contained within this document is for educational and entertainment purposes only. All effort has been expended to present accurate, up-to-date, and reliable, complete information. No warranties of any kind are declared or implied. Readers acknowledge that the author is not engaging in the rendering of legal, financial, medical or professional advice. The content within this book has been derived from the mind of the author. Please consult a licensed professional before attempting any techniques outlined in this book.

By reading this document, the reader agrees that under no circumstances is the author responsible for any losses, direct or indirect, which are incurred as a result of the use of the information contained within this document, including, but not limited to, — errors, omissions, or inaccuracies.

Foreword

Christmas is more than lights, gifts, and songs—it is the story of God's love, sent to us in the form of a tiny baby. This book tells that story through the eyes of a little camel, curious and brave, who follows a star to find the newborn King.

Children often see the world differently—through wonder, detail, and gentle hearts. The little camel reminds us that God calls each of us in our own way, and that even the smallest steps of faith can lead us to something extraordinary.

As you read this book together, may you feel the joy and peace of that holy night, and may your hearts be drawn closer to the child in the manger.
With blessings this Christmas,

Tiina Hoddy

📖 Book Chapters

	Page
Chapter 1 - The Baby Camel	7
Chapter 2 - The Big Star	11
Chapter 3 - Leaving Home	15
Chapter 4 - Through the Dunes	19
Chapter 5 - At the Oasis	23
Chapter 6 - Merchants' Camels	27
Chapter 7 - The Three Wise Men	31
Chapter 8 - Joining the Caravan	35
Chapter 9 - The Long Journey	39
Chapter 10 - The Town of Bethlehem	43
Chapter 11 - The Manger	47
Chapter 12 - The Baby and the Camel	51
Chapter 13 - Mummy Arrives	55
Chapter 14 - A Night to Remember	59

Chapter 1 – The Baby Camel

In a quiet desert village, far from the busy markets, a baby camel was born. His fur was soft and fluffy, the colour of golden sand. His legs were wobbly, but his eyes—big, dark, and thoughtful—sparkled with wonder.

The other camels liked to run and push each other, kicking up clouds of dust. But the little camel was different. He didn't always join in. Instead, he would sit and watch the way the sunlight made patterns on the dunes. He noticed how the wind whispered through the palm trees and how tiny beetles left trails in the sand.

Sometimes the other young camels teased him.

 "Why don't you play?" they asked.

 The little camel lowered his head. "I like to watch. I like to think."

Mummy camel loved him very much. She nuzzled him gently. "You see the world in your own special way," she said. "That makes you precious."

At night, while the herd rested, the baby camel would lie awake, gazing at the sky. The stars twinkled like tiny lanterns scattered across a dark blanket. He wondered what secrets they held, and why they shone so brightly.

Though he was small, the little camel's heart was full of questions, and deep inside he felt that one day, something extraordinary would call to him.

Chapter 2 - The Big Star

One cool evening, as the sun slipped behind the dunes, the baby camel wandered to the edge of the herd. The desert sky stretched wide and endless, sprinkled with stars. He had seen them many times before, but tonight something was different.

There—just above the horizon—hung a star brighter than all the rest. It sparkled with a golden-white glow, larger and clearer than any star he had ever known. It seemed almost alive, as if it were breathing light into the night.

The little camel tilted his head. His ears twitched. His heart gave a funny flutter. "Why does it shine so much brighter than the others?" he whispered.

The other young camels hardly noticed. They were too busy chasing one another through the sand. Even Mummy camel, resting nearby, only yawned and said, "It is just a star, little one. Sleep now."

But the baby camel couldn't sleep. His eyes stayed fixed on the bright star, and deep inside, something stirred. It was as if the star was calling to him—beckoning him to follow.

All through the night he watched, until the first hint of dawn coloured the dunes. The star did not fade like the others. It still burned brightly, waiting.

The little camel's heart pounded. He didn't know why, but he felt sure this star would lead him to something important—something he had been searching for without even knowing it.

He whispered into the morning air, "I must find where it leads."

And so, with the desert waking all around him, the baby camel took his first brave step toward the unknown.

Chapter 3 – Leaving Home

The village was still asleep. Palm leaves swayed gently in the early breeze, and the only sound was the soft cooing of doves in the rafters. Mummy camel dozed with the rest of the herd, her head tucked close to her side.

But the baby camel was wide awake. His eyes searched the sky until they found it again—the great, glowing star. It shimmered so brightly that the dunes seemed bathed in silver.

The little camel took a shaky breath. He had never been far from the herd before. Mummy always kept him close, warning him not to wander too far. But the star seemed to whisper to him, filling him with courage.

"I'll just follow for a little while," he said softly, though no one was there to hear.

He stepped carefully across the sand, his small hooves leaving tiny prints behind him. He looked back once. Mummy camel still slept peacefully, her sides rising and falling with each breath.

The baby camel's heart squeezed. He didn't want to leave her. But the pull of the star was too strong.

"I'll come back," he promised, though deep down he knew his journey was only just beginning.

He turned and set his face toward the glowing light. The desert stretched wide and endless, but with every step, the star seemed to shine a little brighter—like it was guiding him forward.

The baby camel walked into the unknown, his heart full of fear and wonder, following a star that would change everything.

Chapter 4 – Through the Dunes

The desert stretched out like a golden sea. Rolling dunes rose and fell in gentle waves, their ridges glowing in the light of the rising sun. The baby camel climbed one hill after another, his small legs sinking into the soft sand.

He paused at the top of a tall dune, panting. The wind tugged at his fur, carrying with it the dry, dusty smell of the desert. Behind him, the village was already far away, just a faint shape in the distance.

For a moment, the little camel felt very small and very alone. "Maybe I should turn back," he thought. His ears drooped, and his chest felt heavy. But then he looked up. The star still burned brightly, even in daylight. Its steady light filled him with courage.

Step by step, he pressed on. He noticed things along the way that others might have missed: the delicate lines where beetles had crawled across the sand, the shimmer of heat that made the horizon dance, the soft whoosh of the wind as it sculpted new ridges on the dunes.

Sometimes he stumbled, and the sand slid under his hooves. Sometimes he wished Mummy camel was walking beside him. But each time doubt crept in, he lifted his eyes to the star and kept going.

As the sun climbed higher, the desert grew hot. The little camel's mouth felt dry, and his legs ached. Just when he thought he couldn't take another step, he spotted something glimmering in the distance.

An oasis.

His heart leapt with hope. Cool water, tall palms, and the promise of rest lay ahead. The star still shone above him, and now it seemed to smile.

The baby camel hurried forward, eager for the relief waiting among the trees.

Chapter 5 – At the Oasis

The baby camel stumbled into the shade of tall palm trees, his sides heaving with each breath. The oasis sparkled before him like a jewel in the desert—a pool of clear, cool water surrounded by green leaves and sweet grass.

He lowered his head and drank deeply. The water was crisp and refreshing, trickling down his dry throat. For the first time since leaving home, he felt strong again.

Birds darted overhead, their wings flashing in the sunlight. A frog plopped into the pool, rippling the surface. The little camel watched with wide eyes, fascinated by every sound and movement.

Just then, he heard the heavy thud of hooves. From behind the palms came a line of tall, proud camels. Their backs were piled high with baskets and jars, ropes dangling at their sides.

The merchants' camels paused at the pool, slurping noisily. One of them noticed the baby camel and chuckled. "Well, look at this little wanderer! Where's your herd, tiny one?"

The baby camel lowered his head shyly. "I'm following the star," he said softly.

The camels laughed. "A star? Silly thing! Stars are too far away. We follow our masters and carry their goods to sell in the towns. That's real work."

But the baby camel didn't argue. He looked up again at the shining light in the sky. It still burned brightly, steady and sure. His heart whispered, This is my path, even if they don't understand.

When the merchants' camels finished drinking, they moved on, their loads swaying as they disappeared into the desert.

The little camel stood quietly by the water, feeling the pull of the star once more. He was only small, and the desert was so big. But something inside told him he was not lost. He was being led.

After one last sip, he lifted his head high, shook the dust from his fur, and stepped back onto the golden sand. The star still waited, and so did his journey.

.

Chapter 6 – Merchants' Camels

The desert road grew busier as the little camel followed the star. Before long, he came upon another group of camels, larger and stronger than any he had seen before. Their backs were stacked with carpets, spices, and shiny pots that clinked as they walked.

The merchants who owned them shouted to one another, waving their arms as they bargained and laughed. The smell of rich spices—cinnamon, myrrh, and pepper—drifted from the baskets and made the little camel's nose twitch.

One tall camel noticed him trotting alongside. "Ho there, little one! You don't look like you belong to anyone. Where are you headed with no load to carry?"

The baby camel lifted his head shyly. "I'm following the star," he said.

The big camel snorted. "The star? That's nonsense. Real camels carry heavy loads. Real camels serve their masters. That is our purpose."

Another chimed in, "Don't waste your time chasing lights in the sky, little dreamer. You'll never keep up."

The little camel's ears drooped for a moment. Their words stung, but he kept his eyes on the glowing star above. It still shone steady, as if reminding him, Keep going. Don't give up.

He whispered softly, "Maybe I'm small. Maybe I'm different. But I know this star is leading me somewhere important."

The merchants' camels soon lumbered ahead, their loads swaying, their bells jingling in the hot air. Dust rose behind them until they were only shadows on the horizon.

The baby camel stopped for a moment, the desert suddenly quiet again. His heart felt heavy with doubt. "What if they're right?" he thought. "What if I don't belong anywhere?"

Then he lifted his eyes once more. The star still glowed, bright and constant, waiting for him.

The little camel took a deep breath. His steps were slower, but his heart was steady. "I may not be like the others," he whispered, "but I will follow the star."

And so he continued, alone but not lost, toward the light.

Chapter 7 – The Three Wise Men

Night fell over the desert, and the baby camel's hooves sank into the cool sand. He shivered as the air grew colder. The star above shone brighter than ever, casting silver light over the dunes.

Up ahead, he spotted a flicker of firelight. Curious, he crept closer. To his surprise, three majestic camels stood resting by a campfire. Their saddles were draped in rich cloth, and on their backs they carried treasures wrapped in silks—heavy chests of gold, jars of sweet-smelling oils, and shining bundles tied with rope.

Beside the camels sat three men, dressed in fine robes and turbans. They studied maps and scrolls by the fire, their faces glowing in the light.

The baby camel's eyes widened. He had never seen such grandeur. He took a hesitant step closer.

One of the tall camels noticed him and chuckled. "Well, little wanderer, what brings you here?"

"I'm following the star," the baby camel said quietly, pointing his nose to the sky.

"The three great camels lifted their heads to look. Their masters did the same. The star shimmered above them, brighter than all the others.

"Ah," one wise man murmured. "The child understands. We too are following the star."

The baby camel's heart leapt. "You are?"

"Yes," the grand camel said kindly. "Our masters believe it will lead us to a newborn King. They have brought gifts to honour Him."

The little camel's eyes sparkled. For the first time, he didn't feel silly or alone. These travelers believed in the star too.

"Come," said another of the tall camels, lowering his head. "Journey with us. The road is long, but together we are stronger."

The baby camel stepped closer to the firelight, warmth filling his heart. At last, he had found others who understood.

That night, as the caravan moved forward under the glowing star, the little camel walked proudly among the great camels, no longer just a wanderer, but part of something wondrous.

Chapter 8 – Joining the Caravan

The desert night stretched wide and silent, but the caravan of camels moved with steady purpose. The baby camel trotted close beside the largest of them, his little hooves leaving small prints next to their big, heavy tracks.

For the first time since leaving home, he didn't feel so alone. The great camels carried treasures fit for a king—chests of gold, jars of frankincense, and bundles of myrrh. Their saddles jingled with bells that chimed softly as they walked.

The baby camel carried nothing at all. His back was bare, his steps light. He wondered if he truly belonged.

One of the tall camels bent his long neck down and spoke kindly. "Do not worry, little one. You may not carry gifts on your back, but you are carrying something just as precious."

The baby camel blinked. "What do you mean?"

"You carry a heart that believes," the tall camel said. "That is a gift no one else can bring."

The words filled the little camel with warmth. He lifted his head and looked again at the star, gleaming brighter than ever.

The wise men's voices drifted through the air as they spoke quietly to one another. "We are close now," one said. "The star is guiding us to a child… a King."

The baby camel's ears perked up. A King? A baby? His heart fluttered. Perhaps this was why the star had called him from so far away.

As dawn painted the desert sky pink and gold, the caravan pressed on. The little camel walked proudly in their midst, his steps light but steady. For the first time in his life, he felt he was exactly where he was meant to be.

Chapter 9 – The Long Journey

Day after day, the caravan moved across the endless desert. The sun blazed hot in the sky, and the sand shimmered like fire. At night the air turned cold, and the little camel huddled close to the great camels for warmth.

Sometimes his legs ached so much that he thought he could not take another step. His hooves felt heavy, and the dunes seemed never-ending. "It's too far," he whispered more than once. "I'll never make it."

But each time, he lifted his eyes to the star. It never wavered. It never dimmed. It shone as if whispering, Keep going. You are not alone.

The older camels encouraged him too. "Steady now, little one," they said kindly. "Every step brings us closer."

"Along the way, the baby camel noticed things the others did not: the way the wind painted ripples on the sand, the cool shade that appeared for just a moment when a cloud passed by, the sound of his own hooves making a steady beat—like a drum guiding him forward.

One night, as the wise men studied their scrolls by the fire, the little camel lay awake, staring at the star. He thought about his mummy, far away at home. He missed her deeply, but the star's light comforted him.

"Please let me be strong," he whispered into the quiet night.

Morning came, and though his legs still ached, he stood tall. The star glowed brighter than ever, and he knew it was leading them to something wonderful.

The journey was long, but the little camel pressed on, step after step, carrying not treasures of gold or spices, but a brave heart filled with hope.

Chapter 10 – The Town of Bethlehem

At last, after many long days and nights, the caravan crested a hill. Below lay a bustling town, its streets alive with noise and light. The baby camel had never seen so many people in one place.

Merchants shouted their wares, donkeys brayed, children ran through the narrow alleys, and carts rattled along the cobblestones. The smells of baking bread and roasting meat filled the air.

The little camel's eyes grew wide. "Is this where the star has led us?"

One of the wise men pointed upward. The star burned brighter than ever, hanging directly over the town. "Bethlehem," he said softly. "Here we will find Him."

The caravan wove slowly through the crowded streets. The baby camel squeezed between the larger camels, careful not to get lost. People stopped and stared at the three richly dressed men and their noble animals. Some whispered, some bowed, but most hurried on with their busy errands.

The little camel sniffed the air. It was exciting, but also overwhelming. The noise made his ears twitch, and the press of people made him long for the quiet desert.

He stumbled on a loose stone, and for a moment he wished his mummy were beside him. But when he lifted his head, the star still shone above, steady and calm.

The caravan passed inns that were already crowded, doors shut tight with weary travelers inside. There seemed to be no place for them to stop. The baby camel wondered, "Where could a king be born in such a busy, noisy place?"

Then, just beyond the town, the star's light seemed to rest over a quiet stable. The air grew still, as if the whole world was holding its breath.

The wise men exchanged a knowing glance. "There," one whispered. "That is where the child will be."

The little camel's heart thudded with excitement. The journey was not over yet, but the light of the star was guiding them to something holy.

Chapter 11 – The Manger

The caravan slowed as they left the noisy streets behind. The star's glow rested gently over a small, humble stable. Its wooden roof was rough, its walls simple, and the sound of animals drifted softly into the night.

The baby camel's hooves crunched on the straw scattered outside. His heart beat fast. Could this really be the place the star had led him to?

Inside, the stable was warm and quiet. A gentle donkey shifted in the corner. A cow lowed softly. And there, in the center, lay a tiny baby in a manger filled with hay. His mother, Mary, knelt beside Him, her eyes shining with love. Joseph stood close by, watchful and steady.

The little camel stared, his breath caught in his chest. This was no ordinary child. Though the baby was small, His presence filled the room with peace and light. The little camel felt it deep in his heart, stronger than anything he had ever known.

The three wise men entered, bowing low. They placed their gifts before the child: gold for a king, frankincense for worship, and myrrh for what was yet to come. Their voices were hushed with awe.

The little camel stepped forward carefully, his eyes fixed on the tiny baby. For a moment, it felt as though Jesus was looking right back at him—as if He could see his heart, his questions, his fears, and his longing.

And in that gaze, the little camel felt understood. He didn't need to explain why he had followed the star. The child in the manger already knew.

The baby camel knelt, his small legs folding beneath him. He had no treasures to give, but he offered the only gift he had: his wonder, his faith, and his journey.

Chapter 12 – The Baby and the Camel

The stable was still, the air filled with the soft rustle of animals settling into the straw. The wise men whispered their prayers, Mary hummed a quiet lullaby, and the star's light streamed gently through the cracks in the roof.

The little camel stayed close to the manger. He lowered his head until his nose brushed the edge of the wooden trough. The sweet smell of hay mingled with the soft warmth of the tiny baby lying there.

Jesus stirred, His tiny hands waving gently. His eyes opened just for a moment, and they seemed to sparkle like the star itself.

"The little camel felt his heart leap. In those eyes, he felt something he had never felt before—complete peace. It was as if the baby could see deep inside him: his worries, his loneliness, the way he often felt different from the others. And yet, instead of feeling small or strange, he felt perfectly known and perfectly loved.

"You understand me," the little camel whispered softly. "You know why I came."

For a while, he simply watched, breathing in the quiet wonder of the moment. He had no golden gift, no sweet-smelling spice, no precious oil to offer. But kneeling there, he realised he had given something else—his trust, his faith, and his long journey of hope.

Mary looked over at the little camel and smiled warmly. "Even the smallest, who come with open hearts, are welcome here," she said.

The little camel's ears twitched. He nestled down in the straw beside the manger, his eyes never leaving the baby. In that holy moment, he knew his journey had been worth every step.

Chapter 13 - Mummy Arrives

The little camel rested quietly beside the manger, his eyes fixed on the tiny child wrapped in swaddling cloths. He felt safe, at peace, as if he could stay there forever.

Then, from outside the stable, came the sound of hurried footsteps. The straw rustled, the donkey brayed, and into the doorway appeared a familiar shape.

"Mummy!" the little camel cried, leaping to his feet.

Mummy camel rushed forward, her eyes wide with relief. "Oh, my little one! I have searched the desert for you. Why did you leave without telling me?"

Tears pricked the baby camel's eyes. "I saw the star, Mummy. It was so bright, and I felt it calling me. I had to follow."

Mummy camel lowered her head and nuzzled him. "I was so worried. But… when I looked up, I saw the same star. Something in my heart told me to follow too."

Together they turned to the manger. The star's light streamed down, wrapping them both in a golden glow. Mary looked up from the baby and smiled, as if she understood.

The little camel pressed close to his mother's side. "Look, Mummy. This is the baby the star led us to."

Mummy camel's eyes softened as she gazed at Jesus. "So small," she whispered, "and yet so full of light."

For the first time, mother and child stood side by side, their journey complete. They had both followed the same star, though from different paths. And here, at the manger, their hearts were united again.

The baby camel sighed happily, leaning against Mummy's warm fur. He was no longer just a wanderer. He was home—right here, beside his mother, and before the newborn King.

Chapter 14 – A Night to Remember

The stable was hushed, lit only by the glow of the great star above. Mary rocked her baby gently, Joseph kept watch, and the animals shifted softly in the straw.

The little camel nestled close to Mummy, their sides warm against each other. Together they gazed at the child in the manger, their hearts full of wonder.

Around them, the wise men bowed low, their treasures laid before the newborn King. Shepherds whispered prayers of praise, their staffs leaning by the door. Even the donkey and cow seemed to bow their heads, as if they too understood that this night was holy.

The little camel's eyes sparkled. "Mummy," he whispered, "I followed the star, and it brought me here. I don't have gifts like the others… but I gave Him my heart."

Mummy camel nuzzled him gently. "And that is the greatest gift of all, little one."

The baby in the manger stirred, His tiny hand stretching out as if in blessing. The little camel felt peace wash over him, stronger than the heat of the sun, deeper than the cool of the night.

He knew he would never forget this moment. The journey had been long and hard, but it had led him to the One who understood him completely.

Outside, the star blazed brighter than ever, its light reaching far and wide across the world. Inside the stable, hearts young and old rested in its glow.

The little camel sighed happily, his eyelids growing heavy. Curled up beside Mummy, he whispered one last thought before sleep:

"This night will be remembered forever."

And as he drifted into dreams, the star above kept shining, heralding the birth of the greatest King the world would ever know.

The Baby Camel and the Christmas Star

Now you have everything you need to connect your child with the timeless lessons of the Bible in an inclusive and heartwarming way, it's time to pass on your newfound knowledge and help other readers find the same joy.

By leaving your honest review of this book on Amazon, you'll guide parents, caregivers, and Sunday school teachers to resources that nurture children with stories of God's love and inclusivity.

Thank you for your support. The message of God's love for everyone lives on when we share it with others—and you are helping us do just that.

✨ Please take a moment to leave your review on Amazon. ✨

With gratitude,

Tiina Hoddy

"How Many Tiny Animals Did You Find?"

✨ Look carefully on each page and see if you can spot them all!

✨ Can You Spot Them All? ✨

Tiny creatures hide away,
Peeking out throughout the day.
A spider spins, a lizard creeps,
A little mouse in the straw sleeps.

A beetle crawls, a bird takes flight,
A frog jumps high in the starry night.
Look through the pages, one by one,
Count all the animals—wasn't that fun?

www.ingramcontent.com/pod-product-compliance
Lightning Source LLC
Chambersburg PA
CBHW042357280426
43661CB00096B/1146